Animals on the African Savanna

by Joanne Ruelos Diaz   illustrated by Simon Mendez

PICTURE WINDOW BOOKS

a capstone imprint

Some of the most spectacular animals in the world live in the eastern African savanna. People take special trips called safaris to go there and see these animals in the wild.

Race with cheetahs through the grasslands where giraffes nibble leaves from the tallest trees. Watch the busy watering hole to see herds of animals and flocks of birds splash, swim and drink. From morning to night, there is so much to see!

Contents

First light spreads across the sky. On the savanna, birds stir in the shadowy branches of the baobab trees.

A secretary bird stretches its long legs and strolls in the grasses.

The Kori bustard looks for a breakfast of insects.

A hornbill cleans its feathers with its bright casque, or bill.

The brown-headed parrot sets off.

The sun sits low in the sky. On the plains, the tiniest animals are off to a busy start.

The elephant shrew pokes its long nose under leaves.

Groups of termites build giant mounds.

A sleepy aardwolf rests in its burrow after a long night of hunting.

Hissss! "Stay back!" warns the black-necked spitting cobra.

Can You See?

While the other animals are waking up, the aardvark is getting ready to go back into its burrow to sleep for the day. Can you spot it?

It's morning.
Sun streams on
the grasslands
where animals
are on the move.

The cheetah speeds across the savanna.

An ostrich runs across the grass. It does not fly.

A herd of gazelles spring off the ground.

A sneaky pack of African hunting dogs wait to chase prey.

Some animals move out of the hot morning sun and into the shade.

A leopard rests on a branch high up in the tree.

Baboons keep clean by picking tiny insects out of each other's fur.

A troop of vervet monkeys balance on tree branches.

The weaverbirds build their nests with long blades of grass.

Animals keep cool
at the watering hole
while the sun grows
hotter overhead.

A flock of flamingos wade in the water.

The African fish eagle holds onto a fish with its talons.

Hippos soak in the shallow water to cool off.

Wildebeest stop to take a refreshing drink.

Can You See?
African water bugs can hide because they look like dead leaves. Can you find one?

Under the hot sun, animals rest on a rocky hill called a kopje (KAH-pee).

Roar! A fierce male lion calls to his pride.

Furry rock hyraxes whistle to one another from gaps in the rocks.

Clip-clop! The baby klipspringer jumps from rock to rock.

A pack of dwarf mongooses look for a new, safe den.

Some animals spend the sunny afternoon helping each other. This is called animal mutualism.

An antelope gives a hungry oxpecker a ride. The bird eats the bugs that bite the antelope.

A honeyguide bird finds a hive full of honey. The honey badger claws it open, and they both get a sweet treat.

An elephant walks in the mud kicking up insects for the egret to eat. Now the bugs can't bite the elephant!

The plover keeps the crocodile's mouth clean by hopping in to eat the food stuck in the crocodile's teeth.

Animals with spots and stripes graze in the long grass. The sun drops bit by bit.

A herd of zebras run across the plains. Soon they will stop to nibble on grass.

Giraffes stretch their long necks to reach leaves high in the trees.

A baby rhino snacks on grass after its mom uses her horn to dig up a small plant.

The dik-diks look for berries to eat.

The setting sun casts long shadows across the umbrella-shaped acacia trees.

Meerkats peek out from their safe burrows.

The caracal twitches the black tufts on its ears to communicate.

Bounce! The black and white colobus monkey springs along a branch.

With snout and tusks to the ground, the warthogs dig for earthworms.

Can You See?
Safari ants move to a new nest every few weeks. Can you find them on the go?

In the dim light of dusk, some animals are hard to spot.

The ground pangolin's brown scales help it hide while it hunts for termites.

An impala hides in the shadows and tall grass.

A camouflaged chameleon holds onto a tree.

The dead leaf butterfly blends in. It is hard to see.

Animals sing special lullabies as the moon shines in the sky.

Noisy hyenas "laugh" to let others know where to find food.

Bush babies chatter, cluck, and whistle to one another.

Purrr . . . Hisss . . . The spotted genet sounds like a cat when it hunts.

A bongo uses its large ears to listen for danger.

Can You See?
Just like a skunk, the zorilla is black and white and can make a strong scent when scared. Do you see it?

Beautiful Africa

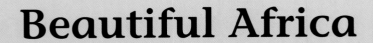

Africa is one of the seven
continents in the world.
The other continents are
Antarctica, Asia, Australia,
Europe, North America,
and South America.

Many animals in Africa are
endangered. That means
there are so few of these
animals that they are in
danger of disappearing.
Most animals become
endangered due to loss
of habitat (where they live)
or because of hunting.

On safari, people
drive around in cars
and see animals in
their natural habitat.
Some people even
camp in the wild!

African animals that
are endangered
include: African
wild dogs, cheetahs,
white rhinos,
and leopards.

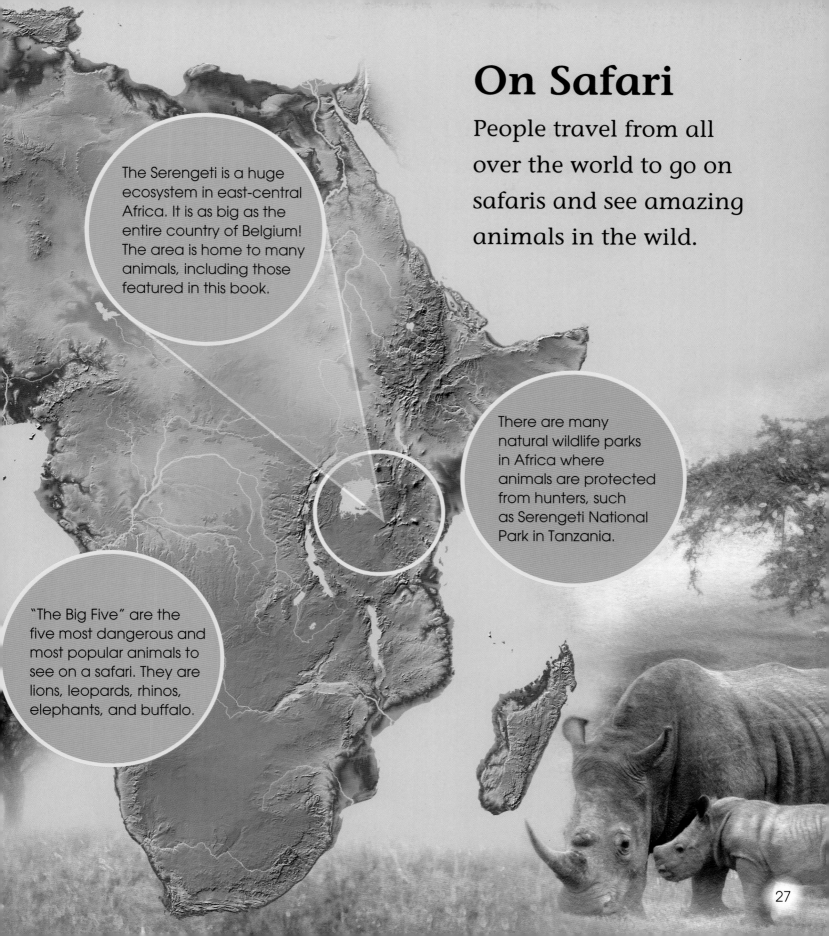

On Safari

People travel from all over the world to go on safaris and see amazing animals in the wild.

The Serengeti is a huge ecosystem in east-central Africa. It is as big as the entire country of Belgium! The area is home to many animals, including those featured in this book.

There are many natural wildlife parks in Africa where animals are protected from hunters, such as Serengeti National Park in Tanzania.

"The Big Five" are the five most dangerous and most popular animals to see on a safari. They are lions, leopards, rhinos, elephants, and buffalo.

Playtime on the Plains

Groups of animals are called different things. Match the correct picture of the animals to each group name below.

1.

2.

3.

4.

5.

A. flock   **B.** pack   **C.** pride   **D.** troop   **E.** herd

Pattern Mix-up

These animals have special patterns, such as stripes and spots. Can you unscramble the animal names?

1. TAEEHCH

2. BARZE

3. DLPEOAR

4. FGIARFE

5. TERBTUFYL

6. LNIPNAGO

Glossary

animal mutualism:
a relationship between two different types of animals that work together to help each other

camouflage:
changing the way something looks by hiding or disguising it

ecosystem:
the special relationships between the living things in a habitat

endangered:
threatened with extinction

extinct:
when a species, or type, of animal dies out

habitat:
the place where a plant or animal naturally lives or grows

kopje:
a small hill in a mostly flat area

nocturnal:
active at night

plain:
a large area of flat or rolling treeless land

prey:
an animal hunted and killed by another for food

safari:
a trip to see animals in their natural habitat, especially in eastern Africa

savanna:
a grassy area with few trees

Index

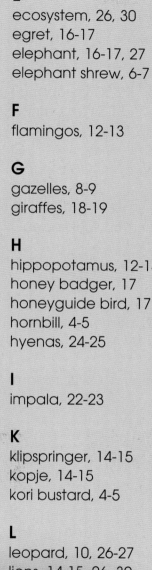

To Lucas, who gave Leo his very first lion.—JRD

About the Author
*A day in the life of **Joanne Ruelos Diaz** includes rising before the sun, writing about anything from animals and trains to princesses and fairies, and monkeying around with her little boy. She lives in Brooklyn, NY with her husband and son.*

About the Illustrator
*A day in the life of **Simon Mendez** includes being bounced or shaken awake by his children, drawing and coloring anything and everything he can think of while juggling the family and trying to avoid emails, telephone calls, and real life—then hopefully finding his bed before the sun or the kids rise. He lives in a small village in the North of England with his wife, twins, and Dill the dog.*

Author Joanne Ruelos Diaz
Illustrator Simon Mendez
Content consultant David Burnie
Designers Winnie Malcolm, Samantha Richiardi
Editor Tori Kosara

Published in the United States by
Picture Window Books

Picture Window Books are published by Capstone,
1701 Roe Crest Drive, North Mankato, Minnesota 56003
www.capstonepub.com

Conceived and produced by Weldon Owen Limited
Deepdene Lodge, Deepdene Avenue
Dorking RH5 4AT, UK

Copyright © 2014 Weldon Owen Limited

Library of Congress Cataloging-in-Publication Data

Diaz, Joanne Ruelos, author.
  Animals on the African savanna / Joanne Ruelos Diaz.
    pages cm. -- (Animals all day!)
  Summary: "Illustrations and simple text describe a variety of animals on the African savanna over the course of one day."-- Provided by publisher.
  Includes index.
  ISBN 978-1-4795-5701-1 (hb)
1. Savanna animals--Africa--Juvenile literature. I. Title.

  QL115.3.D53 2014
  591.7'48--dc23
                                                    2013049252

ISBN 978-1-4795-5701-1

Printed and bound in China by 1010 Printing Group Limited

1 3 5 7 9 8 6 4 2